Geology Rocks!

Fossils

Rebecca Faulkner

Chicago, Illinois

Editorial: Melanie Waldron and Rachel Howells
Design: Victoria Bevan
and AMR Design Ltd (www.amrdesign.com)
Illustrations: David Woodroffe
Picture Research: Melissa Allison and Mica Brancic
Production: Duncan Gilbert

Originated by Chroma Graphics Pte. Ltd
Printed and bound in China by
South China Printing Company

11 10 09 08 07
10 9 8 7 6 5 4 3 2 1

**Library of Congress Cataloging-in-Publication
Data:**
Faulkner, Rebecca.
  Fossils / Rebecca Faulkner.
    p. cm. -- (Geology rocks!)
  Includes bibliographical references and index.
  ISBN-13: 978-1-4109-2752-1 (library binding -
hardcover)
  ISBN-10: 1-4109-2752-0 (library binding -
hardcover)
  ISBN-13: 978-1-4109-2760-6 (pbk.)
  ISBN-10: 1-4109-2760-1 (pbk.)
  1. Fossils--Juvenile literature. 2. Paleontology--
Juvenile literature.
  I. Title.
  QE714.5.F37 2007
  560--dc22
                        2006037065

Acknowledgments
The author and publisher are grateful to the
following for permission to reproduce copyright
material:

Alamy p. **14** (Phil Degginger); Corbis p. **17**
(Bettman); GeoScience Features Picture Library
pp. **10, 18, 35** (D. Bayliss), pp. **6, 21** (Martin Land),
pp. **5 top inset, 5 middle inset, 11 middle, 11
right, 23, 25, 33, 34 right, 42, 43** (Prof. B. Booth);
Getty Images p. **4** (Science Faction); Lonely Planet
Images p. **11 left** (Richard Cummins); Science Photo
Library p. **7** (Alan Sirulnikoff), p. **27 bottom** (Alexis
Rosenfeld), p. **29** (Bernhard Edmaier), p. **32** (David R.
Frazier), p. **12** (Dirk Wiersma), p. **28** (Herve Conge,
ISM), p. **26 top** (Jim Amos), p. **15** (Marie Perennou
and De Nuridsany), p. **37** (Martin Bond), pp. **5, 24,
27 top** (Martin Land), p. **16** (Noah Poritz), p. **20**
(Simon Fraser), pp. **13, 22, 26 bottom, 34 left, 36,
38, 39, 44** (Sinclair Stammers); Still Pictures pp. **5
bottom inset, 30** (UNEP/S. Compoint)

Cover photograph of ammonite fossils reproduced
with permission of Getty Images (Photonica).

Every effort has been made to contact copyright
holders of any material reproduced in this book. Any
omissions will be rectified in subsequent printings if
notice is given to the publisher.

CONTENTS

Fascinating Fossils.................................... 4

Rocks, Fossils, and Moving Earth................. 6

Where Can We Find Fossils?......................14

How Are Fossils Formed?......................... 18

Common Fossils.....................................22

Fossil Plants and Fossil Fuels......................28

Clues Left Behind..................................... 32

Become a Paleontologist........................... 36

Conclusion.. 44

Find out More.. 45

Glossary..46

Index... 48

Any words appearing in the text in bold, **like this**, are explained in the glossary. You can also look out for them in the word bank at the bottom of each page.

FASCINATING FOSSILS

Did you know that some rocks keep a record of the passage of time? The remains of ancient plants and animals that died millions of years ago can be found in rocks all over the world. These remains are fossils. By studying them, we can learn about how life on Earth has changed through time.

Fossils come in all shapes and sizes, including shells, starfish, plants, and even humans. Huge dinosaur fossils have been found in some rocks, and this is how we know that dinosaurs used to live on Earth. Some fossils are so tiny we can only see them under a microscope.

Oldest fossils

The oldest fossils found on Earth are **algae**. They are found in western Australia in rocks that are thought to be around 3,500 million years old. Scientists believe that this is when life on Earth began.

⬇ **Dinosaur National Monument is famous because large dinosaur fossils have been found here.**

algae tiny plants
extinct no longer alive

Some rocks contain no fossils, and some contain just one or two. Some rocks contain so many fossils that they are made almost entirely of fossils. The rock **chalk** is made from the shells of tiny **organisms** that lived in the ocean millions of years ago. When the organisms died, their shells sank to the ocean floor and over time changed into rock.

Fossils show us the types of plants and animals that used to inhabit the Earth. Many of these are now **extinct**, so if there were no fossils we would not even know they had existed.

Find out later...

What do you need to be a fossil hunter?

How do fossils tell us about dinosaurs?

What are fossil fuels?

⬆ This fossil is called an ammonite. It was a sea creature that died millions of years ago. Snake heads were sometimes carved on to these fossils because they were believed to be the remains of coiled snakes.

organism plant or animal

ROCKS, FOSSILS, AND MOVING EARTH

Fossils are the dead remains of animals and plants that lived on Earth millions of years ago. They are found in rocks.

Types of fossil

When a plant or animal dies, the softer parts usually rot or are eaten by other animals before they have a chance to become fossils. This means that it is unusual to find whole plants or animals **preserved** in rocks. Most fossils are the remains of hard parts, such as the shells, teeth, or bones of animals, and the seeds or woody parts of plants. It is very rare to find fossils of some plants, or fossils of animals with soft bodies, such as worms or jellyfish.

Living in mud

Some plants and animals live in the mud on the ocean floor, so when they die they are already buried. They have the best chance of becoming fossils.

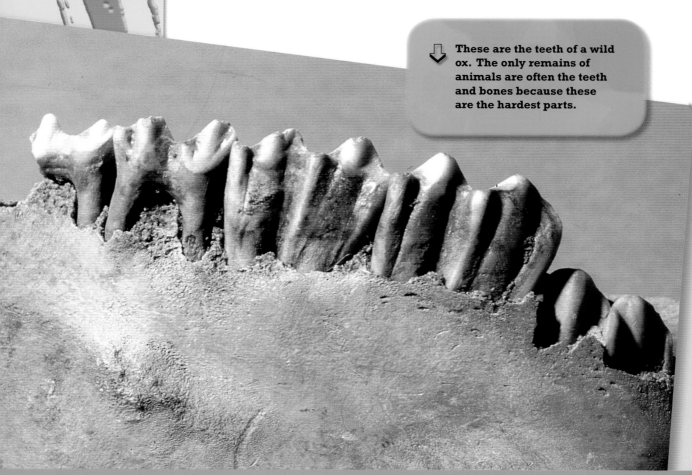

These are the teeth of a wild ox. The only remains of animals are often the teeth and bones because these are the hardest parts.

preserve save something from being destroyed

Most of the fossils found in rocks are animals that lived in the ocean. Wind, rain, and other animals attack dead plants and animals on land, so they have less chance of being turned into fossils. The conditions for preserving fossils are better in the ocean than on land. When animals and plants die they sink to the bottom of the ocean and become buried in mud. They will not be disturbed here because very few animals live at this depth and there is no wind or rain to attack them. Over time they will be buried deeper and deeper until they eventually become fossils.

Fossil clues

As well as fossils of plants and animals, fossils of footprints, trails, and burrows that were made by animals millions of years ago have also been found. These can teach us about life in the past because they show us how these ancient creatures lived.

⬇ Most fossils found are not perfect. This is an **extinct** animal called a brachiopod. All the soft parts of the animal have disappeared, and pieces of the hard skeleton are also missing.

7

Earth's moving crust

Fossils can be found in rocks all over the world. Most of these fossils are of animals that lived in the ocean. Why can their fossils be found on land today? Because the surface of Earth is moving all the time, and oceans are constantly increasing and decreasing in size.

In order to understand how Earth moves, we first need to think about what is below us. The inside of Earth is made up of different layers, like an onion.

The **crust** is a very thin layer covering the surface of Earth. This is like the skin of the onion, and it is where we live. If we could peel away the crust we would find the **mantle**. This is a thick layer that starts at the base of the crust and extends 1,800 miles (2,900 kilometers) deep into Earth.

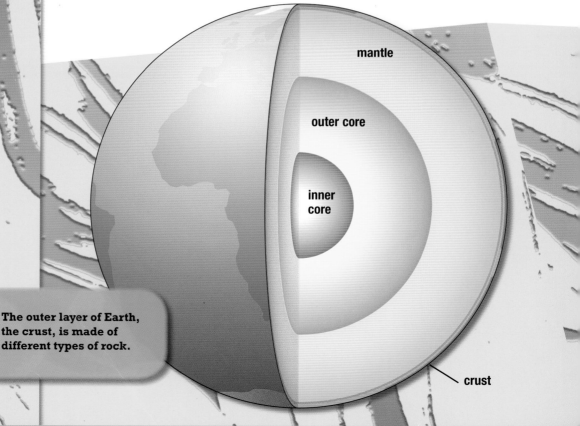

mantle

outer core

inner core

crust

⇨ The outer layer of Earth, the crust, is made of different types of rock.

crust thin surface layer of Earth
molten melted

If you could travel deep down into the center of Earth you would find the **core**. No one really knows much about the core because it is too deep for us to study. We do know that there is an outer core, which is liquid, and an inner core, which is solid.

Earth's crust does not form one solid layer. Instead, it is broken up into huge, moving pieces called **plates** that fit together like a giant jigsaw puzzle.

The plates float like rafts on the mantle below. They move very slowly over the Earth, up to 4 inches (10 centimeters) per year. This is much too slow for you to see them moving.

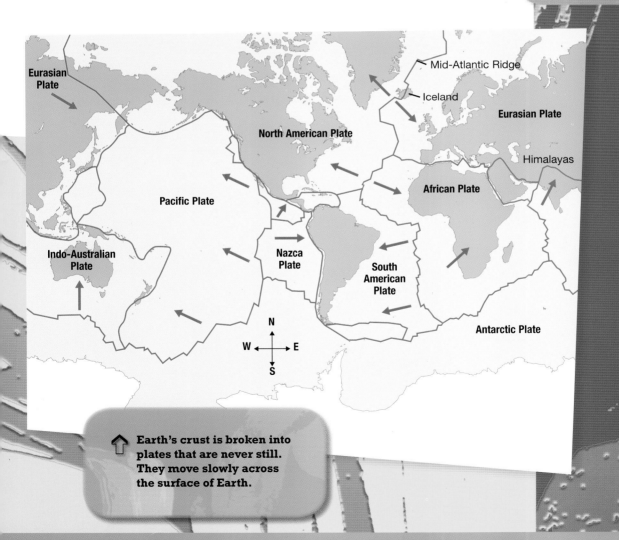

Earth's crust is broken into plates that are never still. They move slowly across the surface of Earth.

plate giant, moving piece of crust
plate tectonics movement of the plates across Earth

How do we know the plates move?

Paleontologists have found fossils of tropical plants in cold areas of the world. This suggests that the continents have moved into different climate zones over time. Palaeontologists have also found fossils of sea animals on land. How did they get there?

When the **plates** move, they sometimes crash into one another. When two plates collide, mountain ranges are produced because the crust is squashed between the plates and is pushed up. Any ocean between the colliding plates drains away, and material from the old ocean floor is scooped up and thrust high into the newly formed mountains. This is why fossils of sea creatures can be found high in the mountains.

Further evidence from fossils suggests that the continents used to be joined together, and have slowly drifted apart over millions of years. The same fossils are found in lands that are now widely separated by oceans. For example, Mesosaurus (a crocodile-like reptile) is found in Brazil and South Africa. This suggests that the animal, when it was alive, could wander over both countries, and so they must have been joined together. A fossil plant called Glossopteris has been found in South America, Africa, Australia, Antarctica, and India, which suggests that they used to be joined together as one landmass.

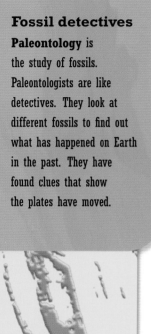

Fossil detectives

Paleontology is the study of fossils. Paleontologists are like detectives. They look at different fossils to find out what has happened on Earth in the past. They have found clues that show the plates have moved.

Fossils like this have been found on both sides of the Atlantic Ocean, in Brazil and southern Africa. This suggests that the two landmasses used to be joined together.

paleontologist scientist who studies fossils

As the plates have moved, new oceans have opened up and old ones have drained away. The fossil evidence suggests that 200 million years ago, all the continents were joined together to form one giant supercontinent we call **Pangaea**. Eventually Pangaea started to break up. This was the time when the dinosaurs lived on Earth. Pangaea split in two, and a new ocean was created that became wider through time. We call the two new continents created **Gondwanaland** (made up of South America, Africa, India, Antarctica, and Australia) and **Laurasia** (made up of North America, Europe, and Asia). These two continents then split again into the continents we have today.

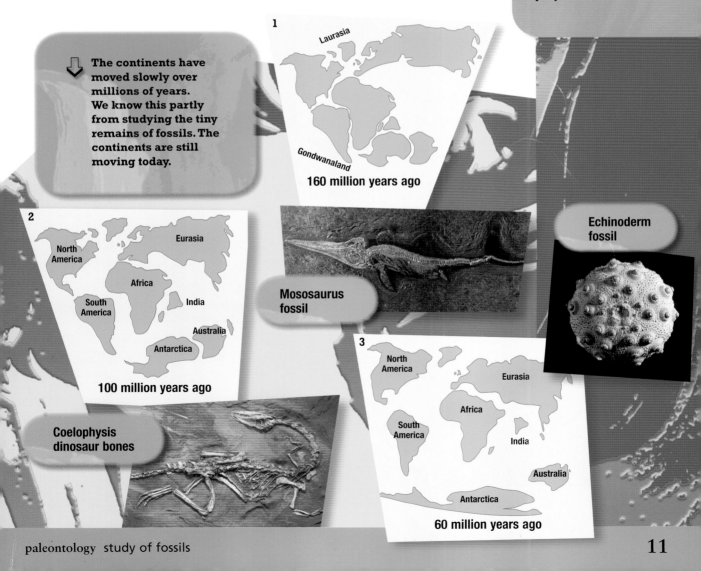

The continents have moved slowly over millions of years. We know this partly from studying the tiny remains of fossils. The continents are still moving today.

1
Laurasia
Gondwanaland
160 million years ago

2
Eurasia
North America
Africa
South America
India
Australia
Antarctica
100 million years ago

Mososaurus fossil

Echinoderm fossil

3
North America
Eurasia
Africa
South America
India
Australia
Antarctica
60 million years ago

Coelophysis dinosaur bones

What are rocks?

Fossils are found in rocks. Rocks are found all over the surface of Earth. You can find rocks in high mountain ranges, on the ocean floor, in river beds, in deserts, under the ice at the South Pole, and even in your yard. If you dig deep enough into the soil you will find rock underneath. All of Earth's **crust** is covered with rocks.

Earth's crust is made up of three types of rock that are created in different ways:

- **igneous rocks**
- **sedimentary rocks**
- **metamorphic rocks**.

Igneous rocks are made from hot liquid material called **magma** that is found in the **mantle**. Over millions of years the magma rises up from the mantle and through Earth's crust. As it does so, it cools and hardens to form igneous rock.

Made of minerals

All rocks are made of natural substances called **minerals**. All minerals contain crystals. There are more than 4,000 minerals on Earth, but only about 100 of these are commonly found in rocks. One rock may contain many minerals.

⬇ **Sedimentary rocks often contain a lot of fossils.**

deposited weathered rock lain down in a new place
magma molten rock from the mantle

Sedimentary rocks are formed from broken pieces of other rocks. When igneous rocks are attacked by wind and rain at Earth's surface, tiny particles are broken off and carried by the wind or in rivers. They are eventually **deposited** in a new place and build up over millions of years to form new sedimentary rock. Fossils are commonly found in sedimentary rocks.

Metamorphic rocks are formed when heat or high pressure changes igneous or sedimentary rocks. When hot magma rises below Earth's surface it heats up the surrounding igneous rocks, like baking a cake in the oven. This causes the rocks to change into metamorphic rocks. When mountain ranges form, the rocks are squashed and buried under the growing mountains. This means they will experience high pressure, so they will change into metamorphic rocks.

Mud, clay, and sand

In areas where mud and clay collect they form a sedimentary rock called shale. In areas where sand collects a sedimentary rock called sandstone is formed.

⬆ If fossils in metamorphic rock are subjected to high pressure and temperature, they may become distorted or flattened.

mineral naturally occurring particle. Rocks are made from minerals.

WHERE CAN WE FIND FOSSILS?

Most fossils are found in **sedimentary rocks**, particularly in limestone and shale. Some sedimentary rocks, such as **chalk**, are made almost entirely out of fossils.

Amazing fossil finds

In some places on Earth you can find amazing fossils. These include rocks containing hundreds of thousands of different types of fossils, rare fossils of soft-bodied animals, or huge dinosaur fossils.

Igneous and metamorphic rocks

Very few fossils are found in **igneous** and **metamorphic rocks** because the high temperatures and pressures deep inside Earth destroy them. Where fossils are found in metamorphic rocks they are often squashed and deformed.

⇨ Sometimes remarkable fossil remains can be unearthed that give us a huge amount of information about life in the past.

bed horizontal layer of sediment

Fossils of the soft parts of plants and animals are very rare. One area where a lot of soft-bodied fossils have been found is called the Burgess shale in British Columbia in Canada. Around 500 million years ago the area was buried in a mudflow, which **solidified** into shale. The plants and animals living there had no escape. They were buried, died, and became the fossils we can see today.

Another area famous for amazing fossils is the Solnhofen limestone region in Germany. Here you can find rare, soft-bodied fossils, such as frogs and dragonflies. The fossils have been perfectly **preserved** because they were buried very quickly in the sediment that formed the limestone about 155 million years ago.

Chengjiang fossil bed

The Chengjiang fossil **bed** in Yunnan in southern China, like the Burgess shale and Solnhofen limestone, is renowned for preserving fossils of delicate soft-bodied creatures. Large numbers of huge dinosaur fossils have also been found in this area.

⬆ The Solnhofen limestone in Germany is famous for containing amazing fossils. This dragonfly fossil is an example of the perfectly preserved fossils you can find there.

Sticky fossils

As well as in **sedimentary rocks**, fossils have also been **preserved** in sticky substances that have hardened over millions of years. These include **amber**, ice, and tar.

Amber fossils

Amber is sticky, sugary sap from ancient pine trees that has hardened. Insects living millions of years ago when the amber was runny and sticky sometimes landed on it and became stuck. They then died there and as the amber hardened around them, they were preserved as fossils inside.

These insects are preserved in amber. Amber is itself a fossil. It is the sticky sap from a ancient trees. As it dripped down the plant these insects became trapped, and have been perfectly preserved for millions of years.

amber sticky, sugary sap from ancient trees that has hardened

Ice fossils

Ground that is frozen all year round in cold regions such as Siberia is called **permafrost**. Fossils of animals such as mammoths have been found that have been frozen in the ice and perfectly preserved.

Tar fossils

Tar pits are large, shallow pools of tar. Hundreds of thousands of fossil bones have been found in tar pits in California. When these bones are put back together they show us that mammoths, horses, and giant sloths used to live where some of today's Hollywood celebrities now live. The animals became stuck in the tar around 50,000 years ago, and because they could not get out they died there and were turned into fossils.

Mammoths
Mammoths were large animals that looked like hairy elephants and became **extinct** about 12,000 years ago.

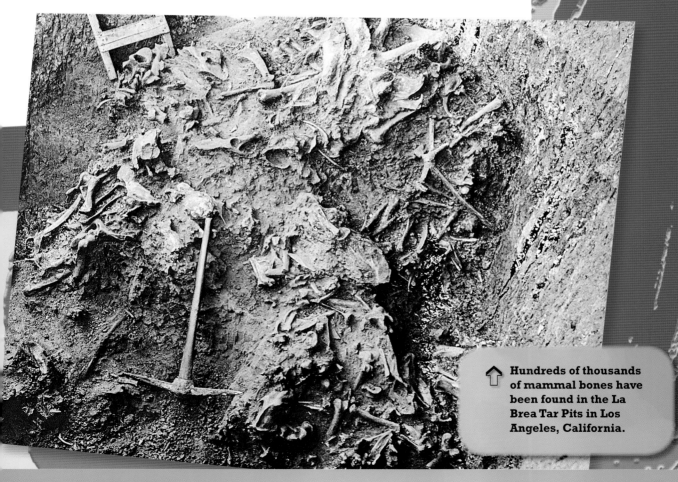

⬆ Hundreds of thousands of mammal bones have been found in the La Brea Tar Pits in Los Angeles, California.

permafrost ground that is frozen all year round

HOW ARE FOSSILS FORMED?

Lost forever?

When a plant or animal becomes a fossil we say it has been fossilized. Most plants and animals have only a very slim chance of becoming a fossil. In fact, most will not become fossils, and when they die their remains will be lost forever.

Changing from a living plant or animal to a fossil can take millions of years. As soon as an animal or plant dies it begins to decompose, or rot. For a fossil to form it needs to be buried before it completely decomposes. The faster this happens the more chance the plant or animal will have of being fossilized.

Fossils form in **sedimentary rock**. Sedimentary rocks form over a period of time as sediment is laid down. If the remains of a dead plant or animal fall into the growing pile of sediment it will become incorporated into the sedimentary rock. This is how a fossil gets into the rock.

If the dead remains are not buried the soft parts will rot away or be eaten by animals, but the hard parts will last longer. However, even the hard parts may eventually be destroyed by animals or scattered by wind and water.

The fossilized fish in this limestone shows that the limestone formed underwater in the deep ocean many millions of years ago.

lithify turn into rock

The sediment containing fossils is laid down in horizontal layers called **beds**. Over millions of years these beds are squashed and compacted as new sediment piles on top. This pushes the **mineral** grains in the sediment closer together. Some mineral grains act like cement, and stick the sediment together so that, eventually, sedimentary rock is formed.

Once sedimentary rock has formed, this is not the end of the story. Over millions of years the overlying rocks will be eroded, bringing ancient fossils to the surface of Earth once more.

Turned to stone

When sediment and fossils become squashed and cemented to form sedimentary rock, we say that the sediment has become **lithified**. This word comes from the Greek word *lithos*, which means "stone."

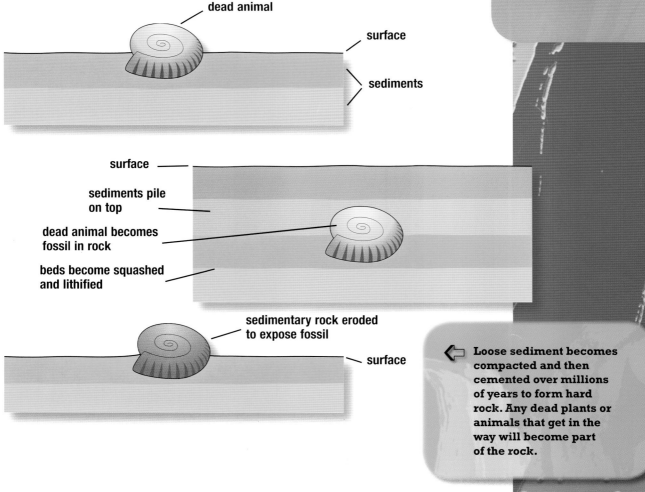

dead animal

surface

sediments

surface

sediments pile on top

dead animal becomes fossil in rock

beds become squashed and lithified

sedimentary rock eroded to expose fossil

surface

Loose sediment becomes compacted and then cemented over millions of years to form hard rock. Any dead plants or animals that get in the way will become part of the rock.

Changes after death

Occasionally amazing fossils are found **preserved** as they were in life. In some cases even the soft parts are still intact. These include mammoths frozen in the **permafrost** of Siberia and insects trapped in **amber**. These are very rare, however, and most plants and animals are altered after they die. Many different changes take place.

Petrification

A plant or animal may literally be turned to stone. This is called **petrification**. It happens because, over time, **minerals** dissolved in water in the sediment around the fossil seep into the fossil. The dead plant or animal may completely dissolve away and be replaced by the minerals from the surrounding sediment, such as calcite, silica, or iron.

Changing form

The shells of animals that lived in the ocean may gradually be changed into calcite. Sometimes the wood of a fossil plant may be replaced by opal.

These are the fossilized remains of trees in Arizona. Minerals have replaced the original wood.

petrification turned to stone

The advantage of petrification is that the replacement minerals last longer than the plant or animal body. This means that the fossils are preserved for millions of years so we can see them today.

Molds

Fossils are often found as molds or impressions in rock, just like the mold your footprint makes in soft mud. This happens when a whole animal or a shell completely dissolves away leaving a mold of itself in the rock.

Casts

After a mold has formed, it may sometimes become filled with minerals that take the shape of the mold. This is called a cast. It is just like making a plaster cast in a plastic mold.

If an animal decomposes, or is dissolved after it is buried, it leaves a hollow mold in the rock. This may later be filled with minerals that harden to form a cast.

COMMON FOSSILS

There are more than a million different types of fossil so it would be impossible to describe them all individually. Fossils can be grouped into several categories according to their similarities.

Brachiopods

Brachiopods are very common fossils found in **sedimentary rocks**. Some types of brachiopod still exist today, although there were many more in the past. They are marine animals with shells, and they live on the ocean floor. They have two shells, one of which is longer than the other.

Because they live in the sediment on the ocean floor and have hard parts, after death they are quickly buried in mud and **preserved** as fossils.

Fossils in medicine

In Chinese medicine, the fossil shells of brachiopods are ground up and used as a cure for illnesses such as anemia and indigestion. The shells used are called stone swallows because they look like flying swallows.

These brachiopods lived in the ocean and their hard shells have been preserved.

Molluscs

Molluscs are animals with shells that live in the ocean, in rivers, and on land. There are many types of mollusc alive today and you may recognize some of them. First there are snails, which have one shell that is usually coiled. Then there are mussels and cockles that have two shells. Finally, there are animals such as octopuses and squid, which have no shell.

Mollusc shells are often found as fossils because most are made of calcite, which lasts a long time. Sometimes the shell has dissolved to leave a mold of the mollusc in the rock.

Ammonites

Ammonites are common mollusc fossils. They look like ram's horns or snails, because they have hard, spiral-shaped shells. Some huge ammonite fossils have been found that are almost 7 feet (2 meters) across. They lived on Earth from 200 to 65 million years ago, but are **extinct** today.

⬆ An ammonite is a type of mollusc shaped like a snail. This ammonite was once a living creature, but now it is made entirely of **minerals**. Fossil ammonites are common in limestone rocks.

Graptolites

Graptolites are long, thin fossils that look like pencil markings on the rocks. They are now **extinct**, but used to live in the ocean. They had tough skeletons, so they are commonly found **preserved** as fossils. Some graptolites were shaped like hollow tubes, while others were attached to the ocean floor and shaped like bushes.

Living in groups

Graptolites were colonial animals. This means they lived in groups (colonies). Because of this, fossil graptolites are often found grouped together.

These are not pencil lines drawn on the rock. They are the remains of graptolites, extinct ocean-living animals.

Trilobites

Trilobites were sea-living animals, but they are now extinct, and are not commonly found as fossils. They were a very large group of animals, with thousands of different forms, and were common all over the world.

They look like centipedes because their bodies are made up of many segments. They also have hard skeletons on the outside of their bodies, similar to a suit of armor. This is usually the part that is fossilized because it contains the **mineral** calcite, which is resistant to decay.

Three parts

Tri means three, and trilobites get their name from the fact that they are divided into three parts across their bodies. We know that some trilobites were able to roll up because fossils have been found in this state.

⬆ Trilobites lived in the ocean millions of years ago. They usually grew to between 0.4 and 4 inches (1 and 10 centimeters) long.

Echinoderms

Echinoderms are animals such as starfish, sea urchins, and sea cucumbers. They live in the ocean, and some types are still alive today.

They are usually divided into five segments, like the segments of an orange. Some are shaped like stars, some like apples, and some like hearts. Some are even attached to the ocean floor, and although they are animals they look like plants. Echinoderms have hard skeletons made of calcite so are commonly found as fossils.

You may have seen a living starfish in a rock pool on the beach. These are fossil starfish (above) and fossil sea urchins (right). The spines on sea urchins are rarely fossilized because they are too delicate.

Corals

Corals are beautiful animals that live in warm oceans, and many types of coral are living today. Corals are made up of hundreds of hollow tubes that form branches and look like underwater plants rather than animals. The tubes are made of hard chalky skeletons, so they are commonly found as fossils.

Fossil corals come in a huge variety of shapes, and are usually named after the items they look like. Examples include chain coral, which looks like long branching ribbons or chains, pipe coral, which is pipe-shaped, and brain coral, which looks like a human brain.

Jewelry

Because of its beauty, coral is often used in jewelry. Jellyfish are related to corals, but they have no hard parts so are rarely found as fossils.

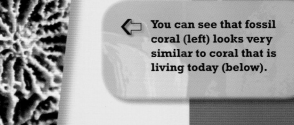

You can see that fossil coral (left) looks very similar to coral that is living today (below).

FOSSIL PLANTS AND FOSSIL FUELS

Fossils of plants are rare because they do not usually have hard parts, so they quickly decompose when they die. When fossil plants are found they are usually molds or imprints of the plant on the rock. This is because as the dead plants were buried under sediment they left their imprint in the soft mud before they decomposed. As the sediment hardened to form **sedimentary rock**, the imprint also hardened and was **preserved** as a fossil in the rock.

Finding plant fossils

Most fossil plants found are types of **algae**, mosses, and ferns, but fossilized flowers and even fossilized trees can be found.

Algae are the most common fossil plants because they often have hard skeletons made out of calcite or silica. They are found as bun-shaped mounds made from layers of calcite.

Plants in Antarctica?

Fossil plants have been found in Antarctica. You may think that it is too cold for plants to grow in Antarctica, but these fossils are of tropical plants. So how did they get there? The answer lies in the fact that the continents have drifted slowly over time, so at some point in the past Antarctica must have been a little closer to the Equator than it is now.

This rock contains fossilized fronds of fern.

Fossil mosses have been found that have roots and small leaves. Some have been found that have grown to the size of trees. The oldest fossil moss is 350 million years old and was found in Japan. Fossil ferns are similar to present-day ferns. They have large leaves divided into smaller leaflets. Some huge fossil ferns the size of trees have been found.

Fossil coniferous trees, such as pine and fir, have been found, as well as fossilized flowering plants. It is usually only the woody parts that are preserved, but some amazing fossils of leaves and petals have been found in rocks such as limestone. The oldest fossil flower is 145 million years old and was found in China.

The Petrified Forest

In the Petrified Forest in Arizona, there are many fossil trees. The wood in the trees has been completely replaced with silica and other **minerals**, and over millions of years has turned into stone (**petrified**).

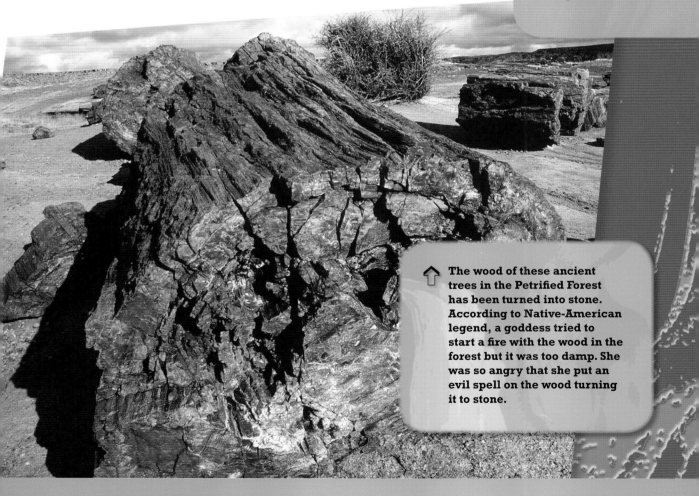

⬆ The wood of these ancient trees in the Petrified Forest has been turned into stone. According to Native-American legend, a goddess tried to start a fire with the wood in the forest but it was too damp. She was so angry that she put an evil spell on the wood turning it to stone.

Turning fossils into fuels

Not only do **sedimentary rocks** contain fossils, they also contain **fossil fuels**, such as oil and coal. We use fossils to find out about life in the past. We use fossil fuels to heat and light our homes, to power our cars, and to make plastic. Without fossil fuels our lives would be very different.

Oil is often found in sedimentary rocks, such as shale. It is formed from the dead remains of plants and animals that fell to the ocean floor and became covered with layers of sediment. Over millions of years, as the remains were buried deeper under more layers of sediment, the remains became squashed and turned into oil.

Creating energy

Fossil fuels form over millions of years from the remains of dead plants and animals that lived on Earth millions of years ago. When these fuels are burned, energy is released as heat and light. It took nature around 100 million years to create the amount of fossil fuel now being burned on Earth in 1 year.

These men are trying to stop the oil gushing out of this oil well in Kuwait. Oil is the remains of tiny plants and animals that lived millions of years ago.

extract take out

Coalfields are the remains of huge forests that existed millions of years ago when the climate was much warmer and wetter than it is now. Coal is formed from the dead remains of these forests. Millions of years ago, when the forest plants and trees died, they fell to the swampy forest floor and were covered with layers of sediment. Over millions of years, as the remains were buried deeper under more and more layers of sediment, they became squashed and turned into coal.

Because coal is buried underground, it needs to be **extracted** by mining to make it available for use. It can then be burned in power stations to produce electricity, or used for heating homes in coal fires.

Coal is mined in countries such as Australia, China, Germany, Russia, and the United States. Before the discovery of oil, coal was the most important energy resource on Earth. Now it has mostly been replaced by oil, and many coal mines have been closed.

Oil

Oil is often found in rocks below the ocean floor, so oil rigs are built in the ocean to get the oil out of the rocks below. The oil is then transported to oil refineries by oil tankers and pipelines. There, it is made into gasoline and the other forms of oil that we can use.

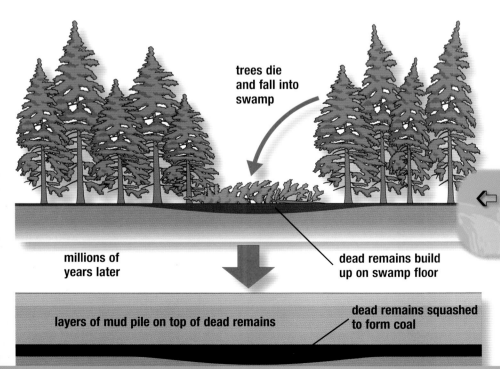

trees die and fall into swamp

Coal formed millions of years ago from the dead remains of plants.

millions of years later

dead remains build up on swamp floor

layers of mud pile on top of dead remains

dead remains squashed to form coal

fossil fuel fuel such as coal or oil that is made from fossils

CLUES LEFT BEHIND

Some of the most exciting fossils found are the bones of dinosaurs. Dinosaur fossils are rare, but some very impressive fossils have been found, for example in the Gobi Desert in China and in some midwestern states.

The death of the dinosaurs

Paleontologists can put dinosaur bones carefully back together, and build a model of the **extinct** dinosaur's skeleton. From the fossils found all over the world, scientists think that there were at least 350 different kinds of dinosaurs. They were not all huge. Some, such as Brachiosaurus, were bigger than a house and weighed more than 14 elephants. Others, such as Hypilophodon, were as small as a chicken.

⬇ **Paleontologists can use fossil bones to reconstruct what an extinct dinosaur may have looked like.**

meteorite rock that has come from space and crash-landed on Earth

The dinosaurs became extinct 65 million years ago. Fossil evidence suggests that a catastrophic event, such as a huge volcanic eruption, a **meteorite** impact, or a dramatic change in climate, may have killed them off. The extinction of such a large number of animals in a short space of time is called a **mass extinction**.

You can clearly see the dinosaur fossils in this sedimentary rock at Dinosaur National Monument.

Gone without a trace?

The marks left in rocks by ancient plants or animals, such as footprints, burrows, or borings, are called **trace fossils**. These markings in the rock are very useful because they can tell us about how ancient animals lived millions of years ago.

Dinosaur footprints have been found in many parts of the world, including the United States, Australia, and South Africa. These can tell us how big the dinosaur was, how much it weighed, and how fast it could run. Similarly, trilobite trails can provide us with information such as how the animal moved and how heavy it was.

Clues from droppings!

Some coprolites have been found that contain the undigested remains of the animal's last meal, for example shells, bones, and fish scales. These can reveal interesting information about what extinct animals ate.

⬇ Millions of years ago a dinosaur walked on this ground and left a footprint. The footprint became fossilized for us to see millions of years later.

⬆ We can even find fossil droppings. This ancient dropping came from a turtle that lived millions of years ago.

coprolite ancient animal droppings

Other evidence left by animals of the past includes droppings. Ancient animal droppings are called **coprolites**. They are usually made of phosphate and are resistant to decay. Evidence left by ancient plants includes pollen grains. These are very tough so they often survive as fossils.

Fossil eggs of **extinct** animals can tell us how many young a particular animal usually had. They can also reveal information about the size of the animal that laid them. Sometimes it has even been possible to cut the fossil egg open to find a fossilized developing animal inside.

Dinosaur eggs

A dinosaur egg was found in Mongolia in the early 1900s. It is rare to find a complete dinosaur egg, and this was one of the first indications that dinosaurs laid eggs.

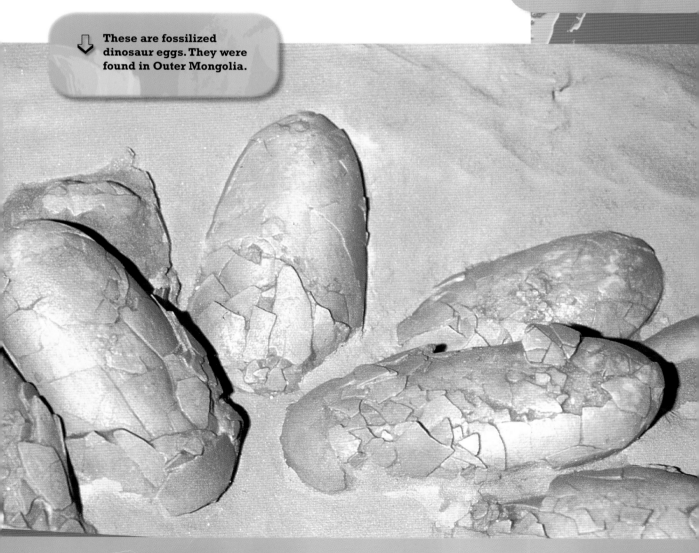

⬇ These are fossilized dinosaur eggs. They were found in Outer Mongolia.

Become a Paleontologist

Fossils are very useful. They tell us about life in the past. They are the only way we know about the dinosaurs and about other plants and animals that lived on Earth millions of years ago.

Evidence from fossils

Fossils do not give us a complete picture of life in the past because the chance of an animal or plant being **preserved** in the rocks is very slim. This means there are lots of plants and animals that lived in the past that we do not know about because no trace of them remains.

Adaptation

The theory of evolution is the idea that plants and animals change over time, as they adapt to their surroundings. Fossils provide evidence that evolution has taken place.

⇨ We can learn a lot about extinct animals from their fossils. This starfish lived 55 million years ago, and was found in California.

evolve change over time. Plants and animals evolve as they adapt to their surroundings

Fossils provide evidence for the theory of evolution of life on Earth, both on land and in the ocean. They show that life originated on Earth around 3,500 million years ago. Since then, many plants and animals have become **extinct**, including the dinosaurs, and only a tiny proportion have survived as fossils. By studying the survivors we can learn about life in the past and how it has **evolved** over time.

Fossils can tell us about past environments as well as past life. They can tell us about changes in Earth's climate, from sweltering hot desert conditions to freezing cold ice ages. Different plants and animals live in different climates, so we can learn about past climates from studying the fossils of animals that lived in a particular area at a particular time.

From ocean to land

If a fossil of an animal that lived in the ocean is found on land then this tells us that the area may have been covered with water in the past.

⬆ These white cliffs, called the Seven Sisters, are on the south coast of England. They are made from **chalk**, which contains the microscopic shells of tiny organisms that lived in the ocean millions of years ago. Because these rocks are now on land, they provide evidence that the environment has changed.

Telling the time with fossils

The fossils in rocks record the passing of time. Millions of fossils have been found over the years by all kinds of people all over the world. **Paleontologists** have collected all the information that these fossils provide to create a record of life on Earth and how it has changed since the beginning of time. This is called the **fossil record**.

Unfortunately, the fossil record does not tell us everything that has happened in the past because many plants and animals died and decayed completely before they could become part of it. Some of these **organisms** are now **extinct**, so we will never know about them.

If the layers in a **sedimentary rock** contain fossils of certain animals, and we know when these animals lived, we can estimate the age of the rock. Some animals are well known for living at a certain time in the history of Earth. If fossils of these animals can be found in the rock then any other fossils near by are likely to be the same age.

Look back in time

The fossil record provides just a glimpse of what has happened in the past, but it is our only glimpse. Without it we would not know about the dinosaurs.

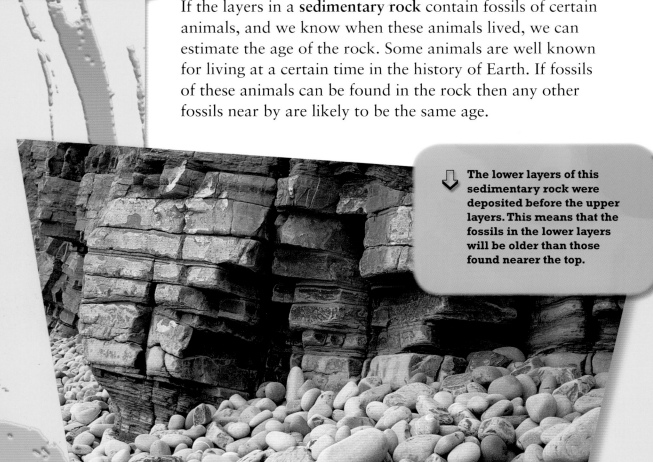

The lower layers of this sedimentary rock were deposited before the upper layers. This means that the fossils in the lower layers will be older than those found nearer the top.

fossil record record of life on Earth obtained from fossil evidence
organism plant or animal

Some fossils are more useful than others for telling time. Animals that **evolve** quickly are more useful for telling time than those that evolve slowly because the change will mark a smaller time period. Animals that are abundant and widespread are more useful than those that are rare or restricted in where they live because these will be more difficult to find. It also helps if the changes that occur are easily recognized.

Ammonites are very useful for determining the age of a rock. They lived in many parts of the world, so are found in rocks all over the world. In addition, they evolved and changed form rapidly. Each type of ammonite lived in a certain time period, so each type can be given an age. This means that if a particular type of ammonite is found in a rock then the age of the rock can be assumed to be the same.

Zonal fossils

Fossils that are commonly used for telling the time period, such as ammonites, are called **zonal fossils**.

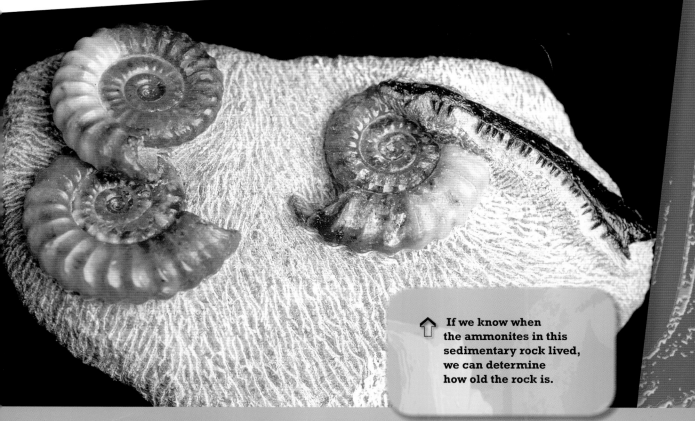

⬆ If we know when the ammonites in this sedimentary rock lived, we can determine how old the rock is.

zonal fossil fossil that is commonly used for dating rocks

39

The geologic timescale

Paleontologists have used fossils to divide the history of Earth into different stages. This is called the geologic timescale, and it is divided into eras and periods.

During the Paleozoic era, brachiopods, graptolites, molluscs, and corals were common. During the Mesozoic era, dinosaurs roamed the Earth. When the dinosaurs died out at the end of the Cretaceous period, the mammals took over. They dominated during the Cenozoic era, and continue to dominate today.

Eras and periods
The different stages of geologic time are called eras and periods. They are determined by the plants and animals that lived on Earth at that time.

Time (millions of years ago)	Era	Period
1.8 to present	Cenozoic	Quaternary
65 to 1.8		Tertiary
146 to 65	Mesozoic	Cretaceous
208 to 146		Jurassic
245 to 208		Triassic
286 to 245	Paleozoic	Permian
360 to 286		Carbonifeous
410 to 360		Devonian
440 to 410		Silurian
505 to 440		Ordovician
544 to 505		Cambrian

Fossils of humans first appeared in the very latest period of geologic time, the Quaternary. Fossils of early humans called Homo habilis and Homo erectus have been found in South and East Africa, and are thought to be more than 1 million years old.

Earth formed 4,600 million years ago. The geological timescale divides the time since then into different time periods. We are living in the Quaternary period.

Main animal life

Mammals

Dinosaurs

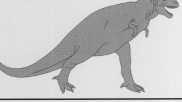

Molluscs, brachiopods, and corals

Graptolites

Trilobites and brachiopods

Finding your own fossils

Fossil hunting

There may be a local club you can join to go fossil hunting safely. They will take you on trips to sites where you are likely to find fossils, and will tell you what equipment you will need.

How would you feel if you were the first person to find the fossilized remains of an animal that lived on Earth millions of years ago? You can find fossils in any **sedimentary rocks,** anywhere in the world. You can even start by looking in your own backyard or local park. You are unlikely to find a fossil dinosaur, but finding fossils of tiny sea creatures that lived on Earth millions of years ago is easier than you might think.

Broken rock from quarries, road cuttings, and at the bottom of cliffs are good places to hunt for fossils, as long as you are careful. You never know what you might find. It takes a lot of patience, and some days you may go home empty-handed. Looking for fossils can be like looking for a needle in a haystack, but you might be the next person to unearth a fossil of a creature that has never been seen before.

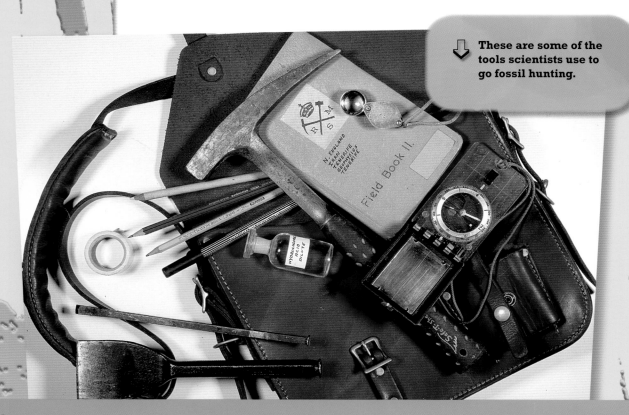

These are some of the tools scientists use to go fossil hunting.

Finding fossils is the easy part. Once you have found a fossil the detective work really begins. You now need to identify your fossil. This may seem like an impossible task. You will need to look in books that have pictures of all the different types of fossils to see if you can match yours to a name. You could visit a natural history museum to compare your fossil to those on display.

Important finds

If you find a fossil you cannot identify then tell somebody. It may be something that has never been found before. You are never too young to find important fossils. A three-year-old boy discovered the first dinosaur egg fragments to be found in New Mexico.

You can look for fossils anywhere you can find rocks.

CONCLUSION

Fossils are the dead remains of animals and plants that lived on Earth in the past. The marks left in rocks by these ancient plants or animals, such as footprints, burrows, or borings, are also fossils.

Most fossils are found in **sedimentary rocks**. It is usually only the hard parts of ancient plants and animals that survive, and most fossils found on Earth are of creatures that lived in the ocean.

Fossils are very useful because they tell us about life in the past. By studying them, we can learn about how ancient animals lived and how life on Earth has changed through time. Fossils are the only way we know about the dinosaurs and about other plants and animals that lived on Earth millions of years ago.

These fossils are called belemnites. They are the shells of **extinct** squid-like animals. In the past, people thought they were thrown down from heaven during thunderstorms.

FIND OUT MORE

Books

Arato, Rona. *Fossils,* New York: Crabtree Publishing, 2004.

Harman, Rebecca. *Earth's Processes; Rock Cycles.* Chicago: Heinemann Library, 2006.

Saunders, Nigel and Steven Chapman. *Energy Essentials; Fossil Fuels.* Chicago: Raintree, 2005.

Using the Internet

Explore the Internet to find out more about fossils. You can use a search engine, such as www.yahooligans.com, and type in keywords such as:

- dinosaurs
- geologic timescale
- coprolites

Websites

These websites are useful starting places for finding out more about geology:

Dinosaur National Monument: www.nps.gov/dino

Page Museum, La Brea Tar Pits: www.tarpits.org

The Petrified Forest: www.nps.gov/pefo

Rocks for Kids: www.rocksforkids.com

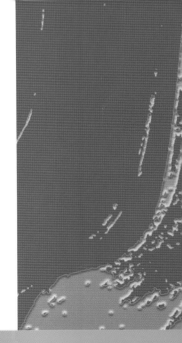

Search tips

There are billions of pages on the Internet, so it can be difficult to find exactly what you are looking for. These search tips will help you find websites more quickly:

- Know exactly what you want to find out about first.
- Use two to six keywords in a search, putting the most important words first.
- Be precise. Only use names of people, places, or things.

GLOSSARY

algae tiny plants

amber sticky, sugary sap from ancient trees that has hardened

bed horizontal layer of sediment

chalk sedimentary rock made from the shells of tiny ocean-living organisms

coprolite ancient animal droppings

core central layer of Earth

crust thin surface layer of Earth

deposited weathered rock lain down in a new place

evolve change over time. Plants and animals evolve as they adapt to their surroundings.

extinct no longer alive

extract take out

fossil fuel fuel such as coal or oil that is made from fossils

fossil record record of life on Earth obtained from fossil evidence

Gondwanaland ancient continent made up of South America, Africa, India, Antarctica, and Australia

igneous rock rock formed from magma either underground or at Earth's surface

Laurasia ancient continent made up of North America, Europe, and Asia

lithify turn into rock

magma molten rock from the mantle

mantle hot layer of the Earth beneath the crust

mass extinction death of large numbers of animals in a short space of time

metamorphic rock rock formed when igneous or sedimentary rocks are changed by heat or pressure

meteorite rock that has come from space and crash-landed on Earth

mineral naturally occurring particle. Rocks are made from minerals.

molten melted

organism plant or animal

paleontologist scientist who studies fossils

paleontology study of fossils

Pangaea ancient supercontinent, when all the present-day continents were joined together as one landmass

permafrost ground that is frozen all year round

petrification turned to stone

plate giant, moving piece of crust

plate tectonics movement of the plates across Earth

preserve save something from being destroyed

sedimentary rock rock formed from the broken pieces of other rocks

solidify become solid

trace fossil mark left in rocks by ancient plants or animals

zonal fossil fossil that is commonly used for dating rocks

INDEX

adaptation 36
algae 4, 28
amber fossils 16, 20
ammonites 5, 23, 39
Antarctica 28
Atlantic Ocean 11

beds 19
belemnites 44
brachiopods 22, 40
Burgess shale 15

calcite 20, 23, 25, 26, 28
casts 21
chalk 5, 14, 37
Chengjiang fossil bed 15
Chinese medicine 22
climate change 37
coal 31
continental drift 9, 10–11, 28
coprolites 34, 35
corals 27, 40

Dinosaur National Monument 4, 33
dinosaurs 4, 11, 15, 32–33, 34, 35, 36, 40
droppings 34, 35

Earth's core 9
Earth's crust 8, 9, 12
echinoderms 26
eggs 35, 43
eras and periods 40
evolutionary theory 36, 37, 39
extinction 5, 7, 23, 24, 25, 33, 37, 38

ferns 28, 29
flowering plants 29
footprints 7, 34, 36
fossil formation 18–21
fossil fuels 30–31
fossil hunting 42–43
fossil record 38

geologic timescale 40–41
Gondwanaland 11
graptolites 24, 40, 41

Homo erectus 41
Homo habilis 41
human fossils 41

ice fossils 17
identifying fossils 43

igneous rock 12, 13, 14

jellyfish 27

Laurasia 11
limestone 14, 15, 18, 23, 29
lithified sediment 19

magma 12, 13
mammoths 17, 20
mantle 8, 9, 12
marine animals 5, 6, 7, 10, 18, 22–27, 37
metamorphic rock 12, 13, 14
minerals 12, 20, 21, 23, 29
molluscs 23, 40
molten rock 8
mosses 29
moulds 21, 23, 28
mountains 10, 13

oil 30, 31
oldest fossils 4

paleontology, paleontologists 10, 32, 38, 40
Pangaea 11
permafrost 17, 20
petrification 20–21, 29
Petrified Forest 29
plant fossils 28–29
plate tectonics 9, 10, 11

rocks 8, 12–13

sandstone 13
sea urchins 26
sediment 15, 18, 19, 22, 28, 30, 31
sedimentary rock 12, 13, 14, 18, 19, 22, 28, 30, 33,
    38, 39, 42, 44
shale 13, 14, 15, 30
shells 22, 23
silica 28, 29
soft-bodied fossils 6, 15, 20
Solnhofen limestone 15
starfish 26, 34

tar fossils 17
teeth 6
trace fossils 34
trees 20, 29, 31
trilobites 7, 25, 34
Tyrannosaurus rex 32, 33

zonal fossils 39